Derang

A Picaroon Poetry Anthology

Deranged

Edited by

Kate Garrett and Rachel Nix

Picaroon Poetry
Sheffield, UK

First published in 2017 by Picaroon Poetry

Picaroon Poetry
Sheffield, United Kingdom

ISBN 978-0-244-60942-9

This book is for those who openly refuse to be chained to the status quo; those who rebel quietly, biding their time; and everyone in between.

This book is for 'deranged poetesses', in practice or in spirit, everywhere.

We Are 11

Dear Virginia 14

How to be a Writer 15

Christina Rossetti talks to God after an illness 17

The Not So Beautiful Pageant 18

Post-sanity 19

Here is how to begin 21

Gone. Sowing. 22

Who have I fucked? 23

The First Time 24

Socks of Fire 25

Short Answers 26

Lead 27

The God of Husbands 28

Wrestling a Cat 30

Girl 31

First Date	32
It Gets Better	33
How to be OK with Being in a Human Body	34
Eye to eye	35
Emily Dickinson Undressed	36
Old and Naked	37
Box	38
Crazy Bitch Who Asked for it	40
Hands and Curls	41
Trigger	42
The Safe Space	43
West Virginia Woman Arrested after Biting off Pitbull's Testicles	46
Antoinette Cosway Reclaims Herself	47
Daisy and the Raccoon	48
Chenille	50
Three Hands Red	51

The Art of Betrayal 52

Yoko Sugiyama 54

Personhood 55

Wasted 57

Sedalia 58

Double Helix 59

Laura Knight sketches the Nuremberg Trials 60

Walking the Edge 61

Eleanor Marx Translates Madame Bovary 62

Lips of Ruby 63

How Tippi Hedren prepared me for Stepford 64

"Attack of the 50 Foot Woman" 66

Writers 69

Previous Publication Credits 75

We Are

for Tara-Michelle Ziniuk

We are women, unnumbered women in the dark,
banking new fire, leaving histories
in our handprints on stone,
burnt hanks of hair, singed rope.
Archaeologists will misname us
when they finger our bones.

We are women, two women in a kitchen.
The pantry empty but for bent
and leaking tins. A time before
refrigeration. The walls are missing,
we step through rubble, we wear helmets,
carry torches.

We are women, two women in a kitchen.
It's the 1920s, we're strapped in, bootlegged.
They'll forget we wrote anything, call
us muses. Everyone we fucked will go on
to the kind of glamorous early deaths we envy.

We are women, two women in a kitchen.
It's the 1950s and we're drinking away our education.
We both wear heels inside the house, one of us in pearls,
artificial. We don't know Sylvia by name but
later her ghost will be compared
to both of us.

We are women, two women in a kitchen.
You wear scandalous pants. The neighbours
gossip about your husband. You are that kind
of woman. We pretend this isn't dangerous.
You don't have a husband.
This is also dangerous.

I am a girl in my grandmother's kitchen.
I hide in the cupboard and watch when
the man I believe is my father
smashes my toy piano to the floor,

breaks it with his feet. This is the
moment I know I'll never be a musician.

You are a woman. A woman in a kitchen
that is a bonfire. You sit so close to the
flames your feet melt. A boy leans into
you to share his trauma.
He might or might not kiss you.
Either way, it will hurt.

I am a woman, a pregnant woman, my body a kitchen,
ankles so swollen if I bend my feet they'll pop
and flood the bare apartment. I stand at the fridge,
drink government subsidized milk from the carton.
Later I will sit in a tub of cold water
and cry and cry and cry.

We are women, two women in a kitchen.
It's your kitchen and I rifle through the
handleless mugs, trying not to set fire
to anything. I don't know you well yet
but I act like I know your cupboards
and you.

We are women, two women in a kitchen.
We pass plates, chop things, graze.
"Kids don't go to work" your daughter says
when I tell her where my son is. She puts
raisins in noodles, adds hummus, cubes
of mango, cashews. She eats every bite.

We are women, two women in kitchens.
You are eating the lunch he packed for work,
I am eating a row of cookies right out of the bag.
It is midnight and we text so often I'm not sure who
said what to which of us but I am indignant on our behalf
while we eat in the dark.

We are women, two women in your new kitchen,
unwrapping your grandmother's heavy candle sticks,
laying dollar store shelf paper in mosaics,

finishing each other's sentences, knowing
the loneliness of being the solo parent
of an only child.

We are women, #yesallwomen,
where the world cooks its outrage,
smoking cars, raised hands in surrender,
all the gunfire that will never bring
anyone's child back. We are
mute with grief.

We are women, numbered women that fill ditches,
stacked like kindling, statistics, demographics,
buried back page stories, hashtags. We are women,
millions of women. This is not a kitchen.
There are ovens, so many ovens.
Thick and ceaseless columns of greasy smoke.

Roxanna Bennett

Dear Virginia

Five hundred guineas and a room of one's own?
No, Virginia, much more.
Even allowing for inflation
even acknowledging historical perspective
even if we could ignore parental script
or hands that slip unwanted up skirts
or somehow
coexist with patriarchy
or Goddesses forbid create
a born-again matriarchy.

Even if one had money enough
or even a house of one's own
or a garden that Vita envied
or we conquered slugs
even if we had a press of one's own
or should poetry become more popular than novels
even if -ist and -ism and -ology were redundant from our language.

Even if we saw the death of wars not loved ones
still and surely Virginia
your stoney pockets and watery grave
tell us so much more –
what a woman most needs Virginia,
without justification or apology is
A Mind Of One's Own.

Sarah Pritchard

How to be a Writer

Grab a sharpie and paint your nose,
your cheeks,
(yes even under your eyes)
with freckles;
write about them.

Adopt a dishonest love for books
and showcase it with your speech;
fill it to the brim with references
never intended to be understood.
Love Bukowski,
especially if you don't know who he died
loving.

Listen to music you will never like
to write verses everyone else
will;
make them say *yes*
when you're writing about saying
no--
glorify your sadness.
It can be innovated
but never
eradicated,
and every chance you get
at it,
is ill-fated.

Fall in love with people you
know your parents will hate.
Love 'til you are out of space to
breathe,
write about the sea
and how its vastness is comforting
understanding.

Write about space and how
the universe is either against you
or with us all in equal
damned

proportions.

Belittle yourself,
praise yourself,
(deny it)
hide,
lie,
cheat
behind your words;
start writing the truth
when it is too late.

Swallow metaphors in the morning,
condemn sobriety,
find depression a safe space
and write about how no one is like the sea;
no one will ever
get you.

Orooj-e-Zafar

Christina Rossetti talks to God after an illness

How reptilian I have become! I draw
these walls around me like slimy depths,
crack open my words before they hatch,
scratch their echoes with palsied claws
until my thick neck twists around silence.
This morning You brought me Summer,
the yellow moon of my head fading into new
light, a cross stitch of shadows and birdsong.
You kiss my eyes with these roses, tap their
sorry heads against the pane. I will force myself
to swallow their beauty, give thanks for the penance
I have paid, my sallow skin pressed against glass.

Catherine Ayres

Between 1870 and 1872 Christina Rossetti suffered from Graves' disease. She recovered, but her appearance was permanently altered. (Source: The Poetry Foundation)

The Not So Beautiful Pageant

There were no pageant winners in my family,
rushing onstage my mother's words pulled me,

fat as a velvet rope segregating our kind
from the beautiful ones. Girls like us should
make shadows our evening wear, perhaps learn
to sew sequins on someone else's gown.

The lights went up and the faces flashed on.
Beauty surrounded us, blondes bright as bulbs.
Miss Apricot County, Miss this, Miss that
twirling the baton of their talent, a tap dance

towards judges with score cards of how easy
they were to love. And then there was us,
the homely who won't stay home, we swirled
not to show our best sides, just what was.

Our soft bellies stretched into tiger stripes,
hair that was teased. Pearly scars, pink
as lipsticked mouths taking a bite out of vanity.
Our smiles unlocked slowly, lips drawn

over horse-teeth quivered free. We stood still,
not perfect, but here, the ones who know
how to take weeds gracefully as a bouquet.
Our only tiaras were the tears of lanky,

plump or strange little girls cocooned
in rooms pale as shells. Tonight we took them
in our hands and wore each one as our crown.

Angela Readman

Post-sanity

We talk about gender like it's binary
as if it is as black and white as that –
missing out on all the glorious colours that are in-between
on the spectrum which they habitat.
Flamboyant and bold and luminous
like neon glow sticks in a cave;
dodging the ugly stalagmites and stalactites of societal norms
creating rainbows as they weave.

We talk about sanity like it is binary
like you're either sane or you are not.
Confusing intellect, sensitivity and creativity
with illness, disorders and diseases you believe we've got.
There is no room for fluidity
in your rigid tick box ways;
open wider your narrow eyes
and real eyes we're not crazy: just post-sane.

Yes we push your boundaries.
Yes we can be pests.
Yes we will analyse your theories
and we will not be repressed.
And when our high kicks and colourful weaving
become too psychedelic for your hairs wisp of peeping eyes,
handcuffs become our bracelets
and you steal the authority over our lives.
But we can work it baby, we can work it baby—
faeries, queers, post-sane and all the rest.
Fluidity can seep and trickle into all the cracks
and lubricate the kinks.
And time goes on and we evolve
into ever more flamboyant creatures;
creativity will be nurtured more and more
and insanity become outdated.

And suddenly we'll realise
that things are not black and white.
We cannot measure 'self' in binary terms
or attribute differences to illnesses and shite.
Sanity is outdated, I'd rather be post-sane

evolving and travelling into the cosmos
drifting away from old fashioned terms and chains.

We no longer talk about people
being just black or white,
and we recognise that People Of Colour
can also have a skin tone that is light.
It seems that society's vision and terminology
is a bucket full of shite.
Gender and sanity are not binary
and the universe is more than black and white.

QWD

Here is how to begin

Response to Ana Mendieta, Cuban American performance artist, sculptor, painter and video artist

Naked, hold a chicken by its feet,
let it struggle just below
your bare midriff.
Do not move, do not say anything.

Take your clothes off again;
ask your friends to glue grass to your back
as you lie face down in a field.
Think of nothing.

Apply a pane of glass to your body.
Rearrange your breasts so that
one nipple is squashed flat,
the other puffs from the glass's edge.

Place a lamb's heart
on your bandaged chest.
Explore gun powder,
scorch leaf imprints into dead wood.

When people ask what you are doing
tell them that gluing single feathers
to each pore of a person's skin
is a work of intense labour
not easily forgotten.

Rebecca Audra Smith

Gone. Sowing.

Even now, there is a certain cadence that rises,
each syllable swelling upward only to be pounded
into a period, that shoves me back into the front
pew and forces breath into years I spent nodding
straight-backed, hands clasped. I begin to slouch
and pick my nails. The labels I have chosen
slide from my body. A bra strap exposed and not
tucked fast enough, they say brothers stumble.
Feminist. Progressive. Universalist. A neckline
that falls four fingers below my collar bone—
backsplash of flesh. Ladies, you need to embrace
your true nature and step back. There's no room
for men if you're out front. Quit taking up space
that's not yours. When women are in charge
destruction follows. Those shrill feminazis shatter
society's foundations. Ugly women and lesbians
are feminists. Backslider. Heretic. Ugly. I bite
my lip. Split. Silent before because I believed
I dangled an inch above the flames. I didn't
fall. I jumped, testing the spirits and nothing
sparked. For a long time after I left, I stayed
hushed. I didn't know I owned everything
that happened to me. I didn't know I didn't
need permission to take every thought captive,
tell every secret. They say I'm sowing discord
in the body, but I'm already gone. Seeds aloft.

Abigail Carl-Klassen

Who have I fucked?

In this room, two. One I haven't fucked
for a couple of years; one I am sitting next to
right now who I did fuck, once and maybe,
looking at the hair sweep the nape of their neck,
I would like to fuck again.

One who I have known for a while
and about whom have debated the logistics
of possibly fucking at some point;
but they are too similar to me and I think I am
bruised enough already to know
the dangers of that.

One who I suspect would love to fuck me but
that one is never going to happen.

One stranger, looking. No chance.

One instant attraction in glasses and I think
fuck yeah.

Jane Burn

The First Time

I lost my virginity to a vampire.
Not a vampire, really, but someone
who sucked blood out of me like one.
It was much better than the first time, too.
The time I lost my real virginity, with blood
all over my party dress. This time I wanted to.
I said yes, let's do this. I came prepared
with a belly full of peanut butter instead
of champagne. I didn't even flinch
when poked. No, I just looked
at my notifications stone-cold sober,
rather than the roof of his car,
fading in and out of drunkenness.
I did experience a touch of lightheadedness
as I squeezed the ball, in and out every few
seconds; but it was nothing compared
to a full-moon psyched asshole werewolf
humping me in a church parking lot.
Against my will. After puking my guts out,
after making it clear I wanted to wait.
No, this time it was everything I expected,
this first time donating blood.

Laurie Kolp

Socks of Fire

Never mind that the manager instructed you to wear solid black or navy socks. *Hey little pistol.* You'll even forget the four fat fucks at table five. *Want to make some extra cash?* You got the round table tonight and in these smokin' socks you'll serve chicken fried chicken, mashed potatoes and sawmill gravy scintillatingly. *Let me be your pepper, you salty centerfold.* You. The star of the Cracker Barrel Ballet and Roadside Freak Show. Your Glowing Charcoal Argyle Socks (No. 555), dyed in China, will stay mid-calf as you dance to the tune of cranky, deep fried okra. *What time you get off? I'm staying at the hotel next door.* Even that 50-cent tip left by the two old crones is no match for these swanky Uzbekistan-combustible-cotton, hand quilted socks. *Another cup of coffee hon*. Your patrons will be amazed as you blaze through kitchen grease seizing oversized portions of mac and cheese for their delight. *More cornbread. More biscuits.* Then, sparks flickering from your ankles—the manager notices your defiance. You are fired. You're secretly thrilled. He calls you into his office. You take a seat. Kick off your shoes. Light a cigarette from your hand linked-heel.

Ribbed, stay-up tops. Made by India's leading hosiery-maker to the upper caste. $13. Glowing Charcoal Argyle Socks (No. 555), as described, combustible cotton.

Susan Yount

Short Answers

My house is big.
As you wander
from room to room,
you ask
where is he?
The man.
The man
who paid for this.

He is a she
and she
is dead.

Lizzie Holden

Lead

We asked ourselves whose lips should go on the outside when we kissed.
With boys, I'd never wondered.
We asked ourselves which of us was the man.
We were too young to know that's a rude question,
So we asked ourselves.

We both wanted to be the man.
I knew I was the man because she would put on a dress to impress me before she came to my house.
She knew she was the man because she put on that dress to convince me to give in to what we both wanted.
I knew I was the man because I wouldn't give her my feelings.
She knew she was the man because she wasn't afraid.
We both wanted to be the one with the power.
We both wanted to be the one with the strength.

Every role I knew broke when I was with her.
Who was supposed to pay at the restaurant?
Who was allowed to cry when we were sad?
Every role I knew I reinvented with her.
What is sex and where does it end?
How does any relationship begin, or progress, or complete?
We were too young to know how to hang on to what we had,
But every role I know reaches back to her.

We could never go back to how it had been before we touched.
Even years later, when everyone had forgotten except for us,
She kept a table between us while we talked at the class reunion,
Reminding me, for better or for worse,
That we couldn't go back to any time before

We asked ourselves
What we both wanted.

Every role we knew,
Every table we could not walk around,
Every role to which we could not return,
Every kiss that someone has to lead.

Annabeth Leong

The God of Husbands

Perhaps, once, when fragments were wholes,
you walked with Sappho along the shores of Sicily,
wet sand between your toes,
wearing nothing but a cloak of seafoam and
pointing east against the setting sun toward Lesbos
you said *Look at he who severs us, forgetting*
how love first was born and wrecked alone upon the beach,
dirty, half-drowned, wrapped up in a fisherman's net
and not one of them there to show her how to breathe,
and perhaps she, in exchange, imagined that vision
to be you, though the thought itself was blasphemy
to imbue a mortal woman with divinity
but this was everything she knew of wanting
and she saw exile marked by the hand that divided
the last of the light from the encroaching night –

if for husbands, this would be enough,

to see, perhaps, Hypatia's eyes rise for a moment
from the parchment that marks the Heavens and the Earth
and to square her there at the centre of the universe,
the movement of celestial spheres come to rest
over Alexandria, over the temple of her wisdom,
the scales aligned for astronomer to work by candlelight,
her gaze turned upwards to trace that path
by which the goddess scarred the sky in her falling,
iron in her wake from which they forged her
chains and shackles, rings and bangles, thrones
from which no judgement passed her lips
but rained down upon her head
as oyster shells from that same net that caught her –

if for husbands, should the works remain,
and lips meet the dampened skin to taste its salt,
to soothe the wound that amputated all desires

for war and craft and sons and daughters,
to kiss that prayer to kindly mother Leto
to graft upon me what it is I lack.

Alas, for husbands, I could have been enough.

Amy Kinsman

Wrestling a Cat

It was time for a bad year
to lap up a saucer of milk
and climb up my bedside.
            In the nursing home,
            my grandmother pointed
            to the pale field in her window—
If you can't see the cow
in the church out there
there's something the matter with you,
you've got no imagination.
Later, I scrubbed feeling
nineteen hours slough off my bones—
the pale paste lathered into a cloud.
            I had seen this all before, long ago,
            had woke to two plumes
            of smoke from my grandmother's
            Carlton 120s, she stood over me—
            you should have been a girl-child, she said,
            the old blood is strong in you, she told me.
            So she taught me to read dice, what a cat will not say,
            and palm prints—the life a crow on my bedpost had sold me.
If a girl, you sleep with a knife in a pail of fresh milk,
you need a high post bed, sleep in your head.
I don't have the ears left to hear her.

Justin C. Burkart

Girl

scabbed knees and messy pigtails
socks in sandals and dirty nails
i stood proudly

they called me a "tomboy"
my mother called me daughter
but i didn't see the difference

while wearing a frilled velvet dress from a 90s family sitcom
i took a live worm in one hand

i never liked bugs
but feeling it squirm within my grasp
i was ready to throw it in defiance
i was powerful

the boys chanted while the girls squealed
and I was caught somewhere in between the noise
trying to reconcile the two sides
of warring tribes that don't know why
pink and blue don't get along

so i launched its gray, wriggling body at the brick wall ahead

the splattered guts made the girls scream
and the boys clap their muddied hands

i had broken the sound barrier

J.P. Grimm

First Date

Women can't drive my car, he said, adjusting his mirrored sunglasses. *Because it's a stick?* I asked. *Because they don't know how to drive fast,* he said. My mind flashed a warning like flares after an accident. In his lenses I saw my reflection and the two roads before me – the girl who could giggle and ignore it or the girl who refused to be his assumption. I held my hand out. *Give me the keys.* I gunned the engine, left tire tracks on the pavement, looping like an autograph. He watched the needle of the speedometer pulse – a thin red knife, thin as the stretched smile he'd given me when we first met. I laughed and pushed harder, foot pressing down on pedal, pressing down on the bullshit line he'd given me, pressing down on every bullshit line every man had ever given me. I hit triple digits – I'd never driven this fast before. I pulled back into his lot and popped the brake, returning him to the place he'd crawled out from under. I tossed him the keys and walked away, left him standing in the parking lot. I reapplied my lipstick, didn't bother to watch him grow small in the rearview mirror as I drove away.

Courtney LeBlanc

It Gets Better

You didn't tell me it was all about the red
ball of the sun, the sucking sky, the doubting orange.

Why am I camping in these woods? O flaming yellow
am I, a fire in my dress of girl-scout green.

The party wild, the artists high, the music blue,
you turn to me, a stranger out of indigo.

You take me to your studio's seductive violet
sofa, make love to me until I shout in violet.

So how could I have known I'd lose the indigo
last night? Kiss me now without a doubt in blue.

We live together in a house of sheaves of green,
sweet-scented flower fields around us sprouting yellow.

Fridays I bring you marigolds and peel your orange.
Hurry, my horse's racing heart is stout and red.

Mary Meriam

How to be OK with Being in a Human Body

Let your leg hair grow for the first time since you were thirteen
feel how soft you are
stop plucking your eyebrows
learn to love how they look when you do
work up to it
fuck myopic men let them tell you that you are beautiful
start to believe them close your eyes feel their body
imagine how wonderful you feel
with practise you can fuck men who fuck like J G Ballard
who take a curatorial interest in the shape of your scars
pore over your pores your wrinkles
who look at you right up close their eyes saucers
who breathe you in deep and when you leave
complain their sheets don't hold your scent.

Anna Percy

Eye to eye

There must be a face
on my breasts.
Some men talk to them
eyes bounce
                down following
their balls
left right back
          right.
I barricade my arms
try
not to jiggle & juggle
rage & laughter.
Raise necklines
voice too.
Fabric looser, morals tighter
makes no difference.
These men refuse
to see me.

Finola Scott

Emily Dickinson Undressed

(after Billy Collins)

Next, he lay my bodice on the oak chair,
collarbones slender schoolgirls expelled
from the classroom of the outdoors.

Each eyelet of my corset was a porthole
the poet met to find an ice storm. I let
my starched petticoats stand without me,

an avalanche folding to spring, winter
unbuckled from the net. Honestly, I know
undressing me felt like he pitched a tent

in the belly of whale. One breath may blow
out his candle, a freckle on my shoulder
could be rust on a maiden ship. Truth be,

if my breast was an igloo, I built it around
a flaming barn. I simply hid it well, one hand
stroking his hair the way idle housewives

practise sewing by taking daisies apart.
Soon, I would be a swan, to him, a raft
of moonlight, a pale stream a sunburnt man

can dive in. Whatever, I knelt by the window,
the afternoon branded to my eyes, a host
of the sun on my tongue, quietly all mine.

Angela Readman

Old and Naked

After Alice Neel, Self-Portrait at 80

She's got one swollen ankle cocked,
like a petulant child forced to pose
and pose. But who forces Alice?

Only Alice. No truth left but spreading flesh
mounded in a blue striped chair,
so she chooses to record

the wreckage. Girl's waist, firm, young thighs
swamped in this mudslide. The face
a bitter, fallen face,

mouth pouting, cheeks jowly and flushed.
Alice's clear eyes look out
one eyebrow lifted. She's familiar

with disaster—a kidnapped child,
lost to suicide. Paintings a boyfriend cut
from the frame to wrap the plumbing. Now, her body

dissolving, she'll do what she's always done—she'll see
what no one wants to see. Paint it.
Leave it behind.

Gail DiMaggio

Box

The color of my box is redwhiteblue.
I got myself a Texan American box, y'all.
Inside this box I do not breathe I do not dare.
I stare down the dimensions that dictate
my stasis.
Stay small.
Stay contained.
Speak immaculate.
Keep it concise.
The trouble is I leak.
The trouble with me is mutability.
In the burgundy King James Rainbow Study bible
with all those notes in the margins
I double lined my favorite verse in 1996
when I was carrying the daughter
I could not keep.

Every good gift and every perfect gift is from above,
and cometh down from the Father of lights,
with whom is no variableness,
neither shadow of turning.

I don't know who wrote that shit down.
I just really fucking love the idea
of a Father of Lights who loves you
like he fucking means it.
You can carve that love in stone.
It ain't goin' nowhere.
My love goes and comes
and falls down on roller skates
and sprawls in its own vomit
on its fortieth birthday.
The love I know like a dog
is Daddy taking his fifth or sixth soul mate
to Africa while his eldest daughter
pays for a Motel 6 room in Brownsville
so that her on and off boyfriend
the Scorpio artist
can fuck her in her ass
then treat her to breakfast tacos.

Sure.
You can put a love like that in a box.
Wrap it in shiny silver paper.
Top it with a cherry red bow.
A perfect gift for a forty-three year old woman
who sees herself as an F5 tornado
roaring through a McDonald's straw.
I've been called everything sweet and sour.
White trash.
Cunt.
Whore.
Slut.
Skank.
Babe.
Baby.
Sweetheart.
Baby Darling.
Baby Raindrops.
Mommy.

My son calls me Mommy and laughs
when I tell him Cougar and Sally stories
and trusts me when I tell him we'll find
Donkey Lady Bridge if it takes us two goddamn hours.
That kind of love is what makes me spit in the face of God
and walk away from thoughts of suicide
in my puke splattered cowboy boots.

There ain't no box big enough for the likes of me.
Boxes are cute.
Boxes are convenient.
I'm nature.
So beautiful in my rage.
Deconstructing all that should have never
been built.

Misti Rainwater-Lites

Crazy Bitch Who Asked for it

Nothing prepares you for the final blow.

You see activists poised like archers
on the borders of their personal space,
victims endorsing their politically correct survival, stories handing out fliers
on the importance of consent

but nothing feels more real than the howl
of your predator, leering at his recent find—

waiting to brand you with the smell of their insides;
what more can you mean in this world
if you are not contained in a monster's palm?

What more can you aspire to be
than the grit at the end of his shoe,
the mucus he swipes with his sleeve,
the zipper he breaks when he's finished?

If you manage to escape, relieved you couldn't answer,
know that your end is coming and it won't
start with your name the way your parents'
happiness does, nor include your favorite color
in your elegies,
hell, it won't even begin to register you
as a human being.

He is coming for you,
to give you exactly what you need:
a release from between his legs,
a smell you will never forget,
pain that will learn to change forms
and cripple without ailment—
the final blow.

Orooj-e-Zafar

Hands and Curls

Do not assume that smallness and curls
suggest compliance,
that my smile says sure,
that my body
would be willing with you,
that these small hands
can't kill.

Lizzie Holden

Trigger

He shoved his hand down
my pants, sunk his caramel-colored
fingers into the very heat of me.
As fast as he'd done it I planted
palms on his chest and pushed him
backwards. He raised his hands
in mock surrender, as if there'd been
a pistol in my pussy.
Sorry, sorry, he said, as if
it had been an accident, his eyes
as wide as snow.
I looked at him, cocked the hammer
with my eyes, inched backwards
as if in a duel.
I should have pulled the trigger.

Courtney LeBlanc

The Safe Space

This is a story about a sexual assault.
But I didn't always know that.
I mean,
I never believed it was my fault.
Well not exactly...
But I'd been
Under the misapprehension
That sexual assault was always about
Uncontrollable sexual tension.
Some lovestruck, lustfucked dumbcluck, (male)
Who (aw shucks) tried and ultimately failed
To behave as he should around the object of his attentions, (female).
We'd all heard the tales.

And I was a Feminist.
Wearing the word like my shiny Doc Martens.
Unfamiliar, not yet broken in
But oh, with such pride.
Because I loved the idea of not having to hide.
And oh, how I tried.
I read Greer in my dinner break and misspelled "wimmin".
Insisted that female spaces were safest.
That girls were the allies and boys were the rapists
And I have to ask now: who the fuck was I kidding?
Because even as the lowest of losers, the lezzer, the last-picked, the lonely, the used for the right answer in lessons then dropped like the last season fashions I wore,
No boy at my school ever did more than use me to score
A couple of points with an insult or four.
The girls?
Well.
I had this idea about feminine innocence –
I think that it must have been cognitive dissonance
Dishonesty in a sense because
I insisted that sisterhood was powerful,
all women were one.
But in my week there was no hour more full of terror,
no Room 101,
no ultimate doom
like the upper school girls' P.E.

unsupervised changing room.

Where Joanne and her gang picked a weakling, a wimp.
The slag with the stutter, that lass with the limp,
a weirdo, a loser, a wuss, down-at-heel.
Someone who'd do for a few week's ordeal.
Like an incredibly not-fun round of Wheel Of Fortune.
No Deal or No Deal.
When my turn came I knew that there was no appeal.

They kicked me.
They slapped me.
They pinched till I squealed.

Then the lesson began and I started to feel

Safe.

And then SMACK on the back of my head and the "weirdo" and "wuss" became "lesbo" instead.

And the teacher
just watched
and nothing was said as Joanne grabbed my hair
and I found myself led
to a pile of gym mats to serve as a bed.
"You lezzer. Admit it. You like it." She said.

And what happened next is a blank, in my head.
But soon after, I screamed and I shoved and I fled.

And I know that her hands went the places I'd read
that the bad men would touch, if their egos were fed.
If a girl was too pretty, her lipstick too red.

But I wasn't seductive.
Well, maybe as prey.

And it's been twenty years
twenty years since that day.
And I'm still a Feminist.
Wearing the word like my

battered Doc Martens.

More comfortable, shaped to my skin.

And now, looking back
I can’t even remember the date.

And I’ve only just realized.
Too late.
Far too late.

That it’s not about lust.
And it’s not about fate
and it’s never been love.

It’s how they subjugate.

And yes,

“They” have often been men.

But it’s ALWAYS been hate.

Sez Thomasin

West Virginia Woman Arrested after Biting off Pitbull's Testicles

May 11, 2015: Witnesses told police this week that they pleaded with Boone county resident, 62, to stop hurting her son's pit bull, but she refused.

Her son has eaten all the meat. She tells him, if you don't leave me
something I'll eat your dog, and so she does. Later, a witness says she
bit Pedro's acorns clean off right there in the front yard. He ran screeching

like a wild Indian. When the police come her son has buried her body,
has hidden her in the garden. She's under fresh wet earth, breathing
through the cut length of a garden hose. It isn't about the dog, his flesh

tearing between her teeth, the copper and spice of his blood staining her
dentures and her nightgown. Her son has emptied a hole in the garden,
has piled up thick dirt to keep eyes out. He has trapped her, has made her

a filthy womb, she has to cut the cord of the garden hose carefully enough
that she can hide in the earth, can breathe until safety comes. There is nothing
left of her, nothing but skin suspended from bone. Her son has eaten all the meat.

Betty Stanton

Antoinette Cosway Reclaims Herself

epidermis, berryskin thin and bruised
you start with dying

beauty / dripping like tiger prey blood
moonlight on white snow red

and maybe grace is walking on the tip
of a single claw, *en pointe* and ballroom steps

firelight madness blazing houses,
you, surrounded by locks

fire raging, cleansing, and you
madwoman/melanin/maverick –

you, bareheaded freedom, you rainsong escape

and maybe unyoking comes with the sound of silence
in the middle of darkness, and you, learning to play.

Rishika Aggarwal

Daisy and the Raccoon

At night, the raccoon pads across the verandah, a quiet clatter,
it pushes open the door, comes inside,
sits on an armchair. Daisy talks to it, feeds it scraps,
turns the on the TV, goes to bed. By morning, the TV will be off,
the raccoon long gone.
She hasn't told her daughter. Tell Carol anything, it's taken away.

Daisy sleeps on fragranced linen and dreams of violets. Carol
sleeps in a pod in the city when she's working,
a damp mattress
in a warehouse conversion by the river when she's not.

Daisy's raccoon is learning to make conversation.
It waits for her to fetch its supper, says thank you
most graciously by way of small snuffly noises.

Carol walks past a bakery on her way to work. The smell of baking pies
revolts her. She skips most meals, but when she's hungry
she indulges in protein shakes, pops vitamin pills. She runs a lot,
seriously, no pleasure, but her body grows rangy and taut;
she looks at her naked self in a mirror, approves of what she sees.

Mother used to make her big fat meals.
Father was a fitness instructor, lived on raw eggs. Carol
played squash for the county, attempting to rid herself of Mum's
suffocating love. When Carol was fourteen,
Father died suddenly – heart attack – while running a marathon.

Daisy's raccoon is growing tamer. It's moved
from armchair to sofa, sits with Daisy, is petted.
It smells of mushroom mulch and orange blossom.
Daisy is falling in love. She's been alone a long time.

Carol turns up unexpectedly. Mum and raccoon
are sitting on the sofa, eating popcorn.
Both look up in surprise. For a moment, Carol can't tell them apart.
She opens her mouth to speak, but nothing comes out
except for a weird whiny sound.

Daisy puts her finger to her lips and shushes her.
The raccoon presses a button on the remote and the TV comes on.
Carol watches the flickering light on the faces of Mum and raccoon.
They look happy.

Catherine Edmunds

Chenille

When Chenille went to a tea or church
or rambled around in Woolworth's, she
wore silk dresses, for she thought to be
cup-measured proper, a portion of silk
dress should be touching land, a dirty
brown wooden shop floor, or anything
else she considered as stable as she was.
Although most of the elderly town residents
shivered at the thought that her behavior
was right next door to odd, they uttered
few comments about this protrusion into
what was referred to as a silent lecture
about how they should be: pure to the core.

So Chenille became their goddess,
untouchable, and a yardstick by which
they could measure how close they came
to riding in perfection's saddle.

The day Chenille died, her clothes closet
that sequestered a permanent rainbow
was open to the public's scrutiny. But there
was another unknown closet that had to be
opened by a locksmith, a tired old man
whose keys had unlocked secrets best left
alone like yellow jackets. As the locksmith
opened Chenille's other closet for the nosy
ones, the ones whose weak souls fluttered
at the end of gossamer threads, a closet
full of gunnysacks stared at them, thick
brown ghosts telling them what she had
been and what they would always be.

Claire T. Feild

Three Hands Red

after Louise Bourgeois - for Jerry

Morning at ten is when you come to me,
soothe adolescent hurt that never healed.
Three hands weave trust and warm scarlet safety.

Lost in spirals; we knit identity,
describe scars of menstrual blood congealed.
Morning at ten is when you come to me.

Three hands wrap adult-child anxiety,
Fingers soothe. Working, the hurting is veiled.
Three hands weave trust and warm scarlet safety.

Clock hands banish brooding mortality;
with your berry bright blood the sky has paled.
Morning at ten is when you come to me.

Hands mend webs... my mother, my araignée.
You cradle wounded hands, ringed and scar-sealed.
Three hands weave trust and warm scarlet safety.

Broken loops knot my captive sanity.
But we repair threads – suspend shining shields.
Morning at ten is when you come to me.
Three hands weave trust and warm scarlet safety.

Janet Philo

Jerry Gorovoy was Louise Bourgeois' assistant for over 30 years

The Art of Betrayal

after "Diego's Eye," a photograph by Frida Kahlo

I.
Your camera snaps at me
like a mouth! How close

you press your lens,
wanting my gaze

larger than life, yet cutting
me down to a monstrous

feature—headless eye,
lusting sphere, my pupil

a target you'll proudly cast
darts at. Don't pretend to play

no part in the picture.
Behind that flash, you, too,

fight not to blink, to count
the others you have blinded.

II.
Just your eye—
no proof you can see

inside me, and no trick
to catching it

mythic, unmoored,
not meant to be paired,

the gleam a matter
of light, not of tearing.

I know better
than to paint your eye

as my world, a rising moon
or a drunken sun

burning itself out,
another self-portrait.

Christine Rhein

Yoko Sugiyama

The steady grunt and bang at New Year
comforted her after her husband
disappeared; she never understood why
women shouldn't wield a mochi mallet.

Her daughter helped her, turning
wet rice as it began to take shape.
The steady grunt and bang, the shaft
chafing her palms, reminded her

of Kimitake, brush flashing across parchment,
slicing through sheets, as though he traded
blows with someone on the other side
of the page. He had a different face

thudding against her in early morning,
the same one he wore when pressing
barbells toward heaven—as if
gods accepted iron sacrifices.

Noel Sloboda

Personhood

So, I have Asperger's,
It's like 'Autism light':
A little bit pretentious,
An accidental slight.

I'm not sure if I'm transgender,
Or just always wear men's clothes.
It's not a political statement.
It's just always what I've chose.

I also find women attractive,
But I don't think that makes me gay.
It may be that I could be:
I might be swept of my feet one day.

I seek definition if it's useful.
If it's a helpful classification.
Bringing understanding,
Alleviation of frustration.

Otherwise labels can get annoying,
They just get in the way –
Restrict the view of Personhood,
Giving one feet of clay.

Because we all have labels:
Daughter, sister, partner, friend.
The job that we perform,
The politics we defend,

The fashions that we follow,
The race into which we're born,
But none should be strictly defining,
Or be the cause of scorn.

Because whatever your religion,
Or your gender or your health,
Irrespective of sexuality,
Racial origin or wealth,

Of primary importance is your personhood,
Your freedom to be free.
To say, beneath the labels:
Essentially, I'm me.

Carol Eades

Wasted

I smell like rotten eggs
and taste like cigarette smoke.
My lungs are clogged
with tar and tequila and my
talents include making a home
out of other people's beds.
I use my body like a currency,
and play boys like a game of dice.
My goals include finding someone
who'll fuck me hard enough until I can hear
glass shattering. I go to church
with my knees on tabletops, light a
candle for the dead in my chest.
If I could I'd drive drunk to
crash my car just so I can feel
something in the seconds before I die.

Tell me, could anyone ever learn to love a wild thing?

Sade Andria Zabala

Sedalia

She drops the spent cigarette
to the dust, not even a heel
to crush it; nothing here to burn.
Nothing but dust and what once
may have been a road. It has been
so long since rain she believes
two gods must be perched above,
wrapped in some sort of lunchroom
conflict, french fries, mac
and cheese, paper plates flung
the length of the cafeteria.
How many days until the sky
will even begin to cloud up?
She zips her boot, shakes
the still-empty canteen,
lights another smoke. Somewhere
in the distance is water.

Robert Beveridge

Double Helix

Butterfly ash gown opens at the front,
three rounds of the diagnostic machine
seeking lumps or nodes.

I thought of Rosalind Franklin
working in dark, illuminating
the twisted ladder of our DNA.

Afterwards, they said she was
aloof
        very focused
                        on her work.

Rona Fitzgerald

Laura Knight sketches the Nuremberg Trials

All the accused wear ear-phones to receive
translations of the evidence of witnesses.
The one she is sketching is bored with it all.

He is intimate with fear's little rustlings, its held breath,
its suck on saliva, the way it burns throats.
She notes how his eyes seem singed,

how his mouth stretches across his huge face.
He no longer listens to the prosecutors drilling
into his head. What he has noticed is

her attention, the questioning of her pen nib.
Her eyes flick from paper to subject.
Goering looks up, stares straight back.

Rebecca Gethin

Walking the Edge

We trail bright verticals pocked with flint,
whiter than yarrow heads, whilst underfoot, lime
insinuates, eclipses my boot seams.

You in your impractical espadrilles uncoil your charm.
I see the pearl in your mouth,
catch a hint of cigarillo.

You gather me in, as I harvest rue for drying –
a fine crop. Your words, I think, will pass as migrant birds,
beautiful for a season, but you will be constant.

Not so – those expert hands have weighed my flesh,
ground these yielding bones to raise your bread
and now you're slaked, you'll drop me

eternally laughing into your eighth collection –
muse an honourable estate: think Lizzie Siddal
to your Rossetti.

Think again.
I'll not be your bricked-in anchorite.
I am the countless beats that stir in this great cliff.

Claire Booker

Eleanor Marx Translates Madame Bovary

London, 1884. She's looking up Prussic acid,
her mind half on that evening and her lover,
the one her father doesn't trust.

Emma sends the maid out yet again
to Rodolphe's house to enquire
if there's any reply to her message.

Eleanor's not sure whether *club foot* is right
and fears she's made the husband
less than sympathetic.

Later, there's a meeting of the Socialist League
and she's looking forward to the paper
from that nice Dr. Aveling.

Carole Bromley

Lips of Ruby

Her lips of ruby:
Sometimes, socially acceptable
Jasper-bronze

Sometimes, enamelled
Forbidden apples

Now, a bruised
Mosaic of pure bride.

Secured, they will remain
a Iolite-blue in a sacred bondage.

Sumayyah Malik

How Tippi Hedren prepared me for Stepford

After the final take of the day, they came to my room
like plague doctors in oilskin capes, beaks full of herbs
and perfume. I saw my face reflected in their heads,

their eyes – a flock of full moons. Long-legged
flamingo boys strutted past my window, clicking
their fingers and calling my name, rusty hinges

of their limbs creaked by, snapping backwards
into the stems of broken roses. How their thorns
pricked me, pierced the skin of my dream.

I stood by and watched it bleed. I left in the early
hours still wearing my tattered dress, my hair
knotted into rope. I flew out of there, unspooling,

my life flapping behind me on rolls of film stuck
to the soles of my shoes, all my happy endings
trailing in the mud. I left everything where it fell,

the script clawed to bits, dialogue splattered
on the walls, my bed unmade, feather pillows
still squawking under the covers for my blood.

I saw myself dissolve in that room, spluttering,
a girl drowning in a theatre of claws and strings.
I ran until I collapsed. I woke weeks later in the quiet

of a strange new place, all the peck marks
and scratches miraculously healed to form
star-shaped scars. The town was immaculate:

beautiful houses like spotless jewellery boxes
where women polished their eyes to a mirror shine,
pretty as dolls. I stopped and shopped and cooked

and cleaned and smiled, but try as I might, I couldn't
glide through that life, silent as a bone china swan,
all the darkness glazed over, my body hollowed out.

Joanne Key

"Attack of the 50 Foot Woman"

—Allied Artists Pictures, 1958

I'm eating an apple and watching the ho-hum horror
of a two-timing husband, Harry, wanting his rich wife,

Nancy, locked up in a sanitarium, far from the fifty
million bucks sparkling in his cocktail, in his Honey's

bedroom eyes. And though Nancy's mad all right—
fuming—her pedal to the metal, it seems she's stuck

clinging to the curves of Route 66, the California desert
in ever-changing midnight hues. The apple sours

as I consider the men who grew up on movies
like this one, pundits and politicians sounding alarms

in Washington today because a woman is fighting—
oh, the terror!—for low-cost birth control. As teenagers

at the show, they might have seen the spaceship
as a cue to edge closer to their dates, its shadow

falling over everything as it hovers now, in the middle
of the road, while a giant alien-man emerges

in all his transparency, his projected arm reaching down,
and down some more, plucking Nancy's diamond,

scratching her throat. But the wounds aren't enough
to prove her sanity, and her anger can't change

the doctor insisting on sedation. My teeth hit the core
as Harry tiptoes toward the bed with a deadly syringe—

that is, until he sees her arm, Nancy's hand gone
mammoth in paper mache, badly-exaggerated fingers

suggesting a 100-foot woman, but no one is worried
about proportions, what with the shattered ceiling

and all the noises of a giantess waking, breaking free
of her chains, busting out of the house for a brazen

walk toward town, her clothes magically expanded
and shrunken into a kind of cavewoman bikini,

people running and shouting, *Look out! She's loose!*
Nancy must have really been a knockout at a drive-in—

her moves amplified that much more—her hand
a bulldozer inside Tony's Bar, scooping up a tiny

squirming Harry, dangling him in the strange
glow of an open field, power lines swaying,

transformer gleaming. And there's no stopping
the whole town from shrieking at a female

monster incapable of being the little woman,
of looking the other way as she repels every one

of the sheriff's bullets, Harry flailing inside her fist,
above her cleavage. Amazing, how the drama stretches

on and on—remains of the apple long since trashed,
and those congressmen just starting to stage

their hearing—when electric sparks set off an explosion,
Nancy taking a backwards fall, succumbing to the roar

of trumpets, clash of cymbals, and, even as the credits roll,
everyone keeps gawking, shaking their heads

at a bare hint of leg, as if it's still too scary to see
the whole character, the bigger picture beyond.

Christine Rhein

Writers

Roxanna Bennett is the author of *The Uncertainty Principle* (Tightrope Books, 2014). Her work has appeared in *Popshot, Slice Magazine, The Dalhousie Review, Existere, Arc, Vallum, CV2, Cosmonauts Avenue, Qwerty, carte blanche*, and many other publications. She lives in Ontario, Canada.

Sarah Pritchard is a Norfolk born U.S. military baby made in Manchester, U.K. Pippi Longstocking like free ranges with dog son Louis-the-lurcher 'turnupstuffing' in the wild. Still personal & political & passionate about poetry strolls & poetry en plein air. Co-host of Sale Out Loud. Published in the anthologies *Beyond Paradise, The West in Her eyes, Urban Poetry, Nailing the Colours, Manchester Poets Volume3, Bang, Full Moon & Foxglove, Rain Dog, The Grapple Annual* No.2, Stirred Zines: *Twisted Tales, Bjork, Winter, Audre Lorde, Desire* & *Women Beats*. Breast- 'occasionally limitations of the love lyric are transcended...Sarah beautifully integrates the themes of the political & personal mutilation into a love narrative.' - Livi Michael, North West Arts Magazine.

Orooj-e-Zafar is never found outside her head; most of her resides underneath her tongue. Her debut chapbook, *Home and Other Debris*, is scheduled for release in July 2017.
You can find her stories and other poems at facebook.com/oroojezafarwrites.

Catherine Ayres is a teacher from Northumberland. Her debut collection *Amazon* was published in 2016 by Indigo Dreams.

Angela Readman's poems have won The Mslexia Poetry Competition, The Charles Causey, and The Essex Poetry Prize. Her latest collection *The Book of Tides* was published by Nine Arches in 2016. She also writes stories.

QWD is a poet and musician based in Sheffield. You can find them on their blog at queerwordyanddisorderly.wordpress.com.

Rebecca Audra Smith is always rewriting the story of Pygmalion kissing his wife to life; we can breathe by ourselves. *Twitter @BeccaAudra.*

Abigail Carl-Klassen was raised in rural west Texas and radicalized on the U.S.-Mexico border. Her work has appeared in *ZYZZYVA, Cimarron Review, Willow Springs, Guernica, Aster(ix)* and *Kweli*, among others. She was shortlisted for the Society for Humanistic Anthropology's 2016 Ethnographic Poetry Prize and was nominated for a Pushcart Prize and Best New Poets 2015. She is a staff writer for

Poets Reading the News and her chapbook *Shelter Management* will be released in late 2017 with dancing girl press.

Jane Burn grows older every day, but also less and less afraid of herself.

Laurie Kolp has poems appearing in *concis, Rust + Moth, Bracken, Crack the Spine, PITH*, and more. Lover of running, almonds, and key lime pie, Laurie is forever in search of the best word. She is author of the poetry collection *Upon the Blue Couch* (Winter Goose Publishing) and chapbook *Hello, It's Your Mother* (Finishing Line Press). Laurie lives and teaches in Southeast Texas with her husband, three children and two dogs.
Learn more at www.lauriekolp.com.

Susan Yount is editor of *Arsenic Lobster Poetry Journal* and founder of Misty Publications. She works fulltime at the Associated Press and serves on the advisory board at The Poetry Barn. She has published two chapbooks, *House on Fire* and *Catastrophe Theory*. Her poetry and digital collages have appeared in *Glint Literary Review, Masque & Spectacle, Uppagus* and elsewhere. In her free time, she works on the Poetry Tarot.
Keep up with her progress here: susanyount.tumblr.com/poetrytarot

Lizzie Holden is a London poet. She finds her poems are primarily about love and loss and their sum: grief. The themes of abuse, trees, dance and breath also find their way into poem shaped forms. Some of her poems are tiny. Her work has been published by Pankhearst, *Picaroon Poetry*, Tiger Shark Publishing, Medusa's Laugh Press, Sable Books, and The Emma Press.

Annabeth Leong is frequently confused about her sexuality, but enjoys searching for answers. She loves the Danish language, buying more books than she can read, and wearing out walking shoes. She is the author of the novel, *Untouched*, and the short story collection, *Liquid Longing*. She is the editor of *MakerSex: Erotic Stories of Geeks, Hackers, and DIY Projects*. Her blog is annabethleong.blogspot.com and she's on Twitter @AnnabethLeong

Amy Kinsman is a feminist, genderfluid writer as well as a poet, playwright and editorial assistant at *Three Drops from a Cauldron*. They are studying for an MA in Creative Writing at the University of Sheffield, where they are a student editor with *Route 57*. Their poems have previously appeared or are forthcoming in *After The Pause, Prole, Picaroon Poetry, Up The Staircase Quarterly* and Valley Press.

Justin C. Burkart is a poet from Northwest Arkansas, and a graduate of the University of New Hampshire's MFA, Creative Writing program. He was recipient of the University of Arkansas's, Felix Christopher McKean Award for poetry, and his poems have appeared in *Plain Spoke, The Emerson Review, The Columbia Review, Art Amiss* Volumes 4, 8, 9, *Surreal Nightmares*, and *Headstuff*.

J.P. Grimm is a scholar and teacher by day, and a podcaster by night. She's also a food enthusiast and cat whispurrer who loves to write every so often.

Courtney LeBlanc is the author of the chapbook *All in the Family* (Bottlecap Press) and is an MFA candidate at Queens University of Charlotte. Her poetry is published or forthcoming in *Public Pool, Rising Phoenix Review, The Legendary, Germ Magazine, Quail Bell Magazine, Brain Mill Press*, and others. She loves nail polish, wine, and tattoos.
Read her blog at www.wordperv.com, follow her on twitter: twitter.com/wordperv, or find her on facebook: www.facebook.com/poetry.CourtneyLeBlanc.

Mary Meriam founded *Lavender Review*, cofounded Headmistress Press, and contributes to *Ms.* magazine, *The Critical Flame,* and *The Gay & Lesbian Review.* Her poetry collections, *The Countess of Flatbroke, The Poet's Zodiac, The Lesbian, The Lillian Trilogy,* and *Lady of the Moon,* honor a cosmos of strong, creative women.

The word 'poetess' erroneously makes **Anna Percy** sound like she writes poems about arranging flowers rather than her cunt.

Slam winning granny **Finola Scott**'s poems are published in *The Ofi Press, Obsessed with Pipework, The Lake, And Other Poem,* as well as many anthologies. Makar Liz Lochead is currently her mentor on Scotland's Clydebuilt Scheme. A performance poet, her summer diary is filling up with festival appearances. Watch out for her in a pub near you!

Gail DiMaggio spent years watching her husband play jazz in a world where no artist ever gives up a day gig. She has refused to become discouraged. Her work has appeared recently in *Salamander, Slipstream, Tishman Review, ELJ*, and *Magma*. In 2017, her chapbook, *Woman Prime*, has been a finalist at Tupelo Press and Black Lawrence and has placed fourth at Concrete Wolf.

Misti Rainwater-Lites survives San Antonio on $800 a month, doing the disability-eBay-flea market hustle. She has books and art for sale, always, and can be found 24/7 at Chupacabra Disco.

Sez Thomasin is an autistic, genderqueer poet living in Sheffield. They have written limericks about sex and gender for Kate Bornstein's My New Gender Workbook and have won several poetry slams including Poetstars 2008, Wordlife 2010 & 2016, and the Sheffield Antislam. They were a semi finalist at the 2017 Hammer and Tongue slam. One of these days they'll do a book.

Betty Stanton is a writer who lives and works in Tulsa, Oklahoma. She recently received her MFA from The University of Texas - El Paso. Her work has appeared in various journals including *Siren, Gravel, Proximity*, and *Nimrod International Journal of Prose and Poetry* and is forthcoming in several other publications.

Rishika Aggarwal is a 23-year-old poet from India. She has been reading for as long as she can remember, and has been dreaming of being a writer for about as long. Her work has been published or is forthcoming in *The Rising Phoenix Review, Vagabond City Literary Journal, Wizards in Space Literary Magazine*, and *Sapphic Swan.*
Find her, and more of her work, at rishwrites.tumblr.com, and her chapbooks at gumroad.com/rishwrites.

Catherine Edmunds' published works include a poetry collection, four novels and a Holocaust memoir. She has twice been nominated for a Pushcart Prize, three times shortlisted in the Bridport, and has been published in the *Frogmore Papers, The Binnacle, Butchers' Dog, Ambit*, and many other places.
www.freewebs.com/catherineedmunds

Claire T. Feild, nominated for the Pushcart Prize by Krater Quarterly, has had 366 poems and 6 creative nonfiction stories accepted for publication in 120 print journals and anthologies, such as *The Tulane Review; Freshwater; Ghostlight: The Magazine of Horror; Folio; Domestic Cherry; Rockland Lit*; and others. Her poetry and non-fiction books include *Mississippi Delta Women in Prism, Southern Women: The 1950s, Indigo Blues* (Origami Poetry Project), *A Delta Vigil: Yazoo City, Mississippi, the 1950s*, and *Mississippi Delta Memories.*

Janet Philo is published online (*The Fat Damsel; Clear Poetry*) and in print. Her pamphlet, *Under-hedge Dapple* (Three Drops Press, 2016) was followed by shared chapbook *Dark Matter 8* with Steven Bruce (Blacklight Engine Room, 2017) Her work appears in two anthologies: Midwinter 2016 (*Three Drops from a Cauldron*) and Spoon on the Tracks (*Obsessed With Pipework* 78). Part of the TWP collective, she also enjoys performance, sometimes accompanied by music.

Christine Rhein's poetry collection, *Wild Flight,* is a winner of the Walt McDonald First Book Prize (Texas Tech University Press). Her poems have appeared widely in journals, including *The Gettysburg Review* and *The Southern Review*, and have won awards from *Green Mountains Review* and *Michigan Quarterly Review*. Her work has also been selected for Poetry Daily, The Writer's Almanac, and *Best New Poets* and other anthologies. A former automotive engineer, Christine lives in Brighton, Michigan (www.ChristineRhein.com).

Noel Sloboda is the author of the poetry collections *Our Rarer Monsters* (sunnyoutside, 2013) and *Shell Games* (sunnyoutside, 2008) as well as several chapbooks, most recently *Risk Management Studies* (Kattywompus, 2015). He has also published a book about Edith Wharton and Gertrude Stein. Sloboda teaches at Penn State York.

Carol Eades is an aspergic, polymath, politically aware, diy enthusiast. They are the holder of multiple degrees in various subjects, and live in Sheffield with multiple pets of various species.

Sade Andria Zabala is the always-angry-at-something mermaid/author of poetry books *WAR SONGS* and *Coffee & Cigarettes* (Thought Catalog Books, 2016). Her writing has appeared on *Words Dance, cahoodaloodaling, The Rising Phoenix Review*, and more. Follow her work at facebook.com/SadeAndriaZabala.

Robert Beveridge makes noise (xterminal.bandcamp.com) and writes poetry just outside Cleveland, OH. Recent/upcoming appearances in *Survision, Loud Zoo*, and *Ghostlight*, among others.

Rona Fitzgerald was born in Dublin and now lives in Glasgow. Beginning with six poems in the Dublin based *Stinging Fly* magazine in 2011, she has been published in UK and Scottish anthologies, in Scottish Book Trust publications and in both print and online magazines. Her most recent publications are *Aiblins: New Scottish Political Poetry, Three Drops from a Cauldron* Midwinter special, *Obsessed with Pipework* No. 78 and *Oxford Poetry* XVI.III Winter 2016-17.

Rebecca Gethin's pamphlet, *A Sprig of Rowan*, was published by Three Drops Press earlier this year. *All the Time in the World* was also published this year by Cinnamon Press. She edited the anthology, *A Poetry of Elephants* which raises funds for orphan elephants. New poems have appeared in *Driftfish* and Ledbury Poetry Festival's *Poetica Botanica*. She has been a Hawthornden Fellow and runs the Poetry School's seminar in Plymouth.
Her website is www.rebeccagethin.wordpress.com

Claire Booker is based in London and Brighton. Her debut pamphlet *Later There Will Be Postcards* is published by Green Bottle Press. Her poems have appeared in *Ambit, Magma, Interpreter's House, Popshot, Prole, Rialto* and *Under the Radar* among others. She was commended in the Poetry Society's Anne Born prize. She is also a playwright whose plays have been performed in three continents and on BBC Radio 4. More information at www.bookerplays.co.uk

Carole Bromley has two collections with Smith/Doorstop, the most recent being *The Stonegate Devil*, which won the 2016 York Culture Award. She has a collection for children, *Blast Off*, coming out in June 2017. Carole is the Stanza rep for York and runs poetry surgeries at York Explore.
www.carolebromleypoetry.co.uk

Summayah Malik from Islamabad, Pakistan calls herself a flying pollen of weirdom // cross-pollinated with versification.

Joanne Key tries to choose the well lit paths, but often ends up off the beaten track, in the woods, outside a ramshackle cabin...

Previous Publication Credits

'Socks of Fire' by Susan Yount was previously published in *Eating Her Wedding Dress: A Collection of Clothing Poems* (Ragged Sky Press) and *Bad Jobs & Bullshit: It's Unlikely That We'll Be Missed* (The Geeky Press)

'It Gets Better' by Mary Meriam first appeared in *The Citron Review* as runner-up in the Queer issue contest judged by Jenny Factor.

'First Date' by Courtney LeBlanc was originally published in *Germ Magazine*.

'Trigger' by Courtney LeBlanc was first published by *SHE Zine*.

DID1868567
#0066 - 150617 - C0 - 210/148/4 - PB - DID1868567